Harvest
from the Emerald Orchard

Harvest
from the Emerald Orchard

An Anthology of
the Emerald Street Poets:

Julia Alter-Canvin, Len Anderson, Virgil Banks, Dane Cervine,
Jenny D'Angelo, Guarionex Delgado, Kathleen Flowers,
Robin Lysne, Joanna Martin, Phyllis Mayfield, Maggie Paul,
Stuart Presley, Carol Rodriguez, Joan Safajek,
Lisa Simon, Robin Straub, Philip Wagner

Emerald Street Press
Santa Cruz, California

ISBN: 978-1-4276-1922-8

Acknowledgment is gratefully made to the following publications, in the pages of which many of these poems first appeared:

Julia Alter-Canvin: *Walking the Hot Coal of the Heart* (Hummingbird Press, 2004), "The Night Eaters." *Walking the Hot Coal of the Heart* (Hummingbird Press, 2004) and *CALYX A Journal of Art and Literature by Women*, "What Hums Inside."

Len Anderson: *Good Times*, "The Gift," "A Note on the Use of Metaphor." *Sand Hill Review*, "Invented by the Night."

Dane Cervine: *Buckle &*, "Every Wound a Kiss," "How to Know God." *Nebo*, "The Anonymity of Poets." *Freshwater*, "Sin." *Old Red Kimono*, "Becoming A Poem." *Porcupine*, "Would You Recognize the Truth If You Saw It." *Studio One*, "The Meaning of Life." *What a Father Dreams* (Xlibris, 2005), "A Rose, a Thorn."

Jenny D'Angelo: *Bellowing Ark*, "Saved."

Kathleen Flowers: *Good Times*, "Intertidal Zone," "When I Get Mine," "In These Five Remaining Days."

Robin Lysne: *Porcupine*, "Roots and Rice." *Heart Path: Learning to Love Yourself and Listening to Your Guides* (Blue Bone Books, 2007), "Honey Strands."

Phyllis Mayfield: *Porter Gulch Review*, "Morning Ritual."

Carol Rodriguez: *Porter Gulch Review*, "Pyromania."

Philip Wagner: *The Anthology of Monterey Bay Poets 2004*, "Construction."

Cover photographs and book layout by Len Anderson.
Cover design by Kate Martini.

Emerald Street Press
2299 Mattison Lane
Santa Cruz, CA 95062-1821

Printed by BookMobile in the USA.

Contents

The authors would like to thank Joseph Stroud for his encouragement and his help with many of these poems.

JULIA ALTER-CANVIN

Reaching for the Goldhot Star of a Song

Last night I stepped out of my body again,
half devil, half angel, half stardust, half mooncry,
half of a quarter of a fraction of a shining thing.

Last night I stepped outside the church
of my body, shattered the thin, stained glass skin.
I shed the gargoyles and the silver bricks,
took one breath in.

Yes, I stepped last night onto a velvet stage,
lifted up the microphone.
        After all those girlhood nights
        keeping the neighbors awake
        and my bedraggled, sleepless mother,
        my brothers banging on the walls.
        All those nights singing myself to sleep,
        singing to the goddess of twilight
                    then midnight
                    then dawn.

I took one more step out of shadow last night,
took one more step out of stone, out of the wall
through the window, reaching toward a goldhot star.

Last night I summoned the twilight chord
of five thousand crickets, the satin breath
of the gardenia, stepped into my spirit
singing.

They Don't Serve "The Usual" for Breakfast Around Here

Among the triangles
I am the rhombicosidodecahedron.
Among laughter
I am the blue bucket poured out slowly, every drop.
Among heartaches
that's me with the first prize ribbons.

And between the cherries I am the kiss.
Between apples, the three-day embrace.
Oranges, I am the full moon.
Inside the alphabet
I'm the polysyllabic dance,
the jump from *M* to *J* and back to *C*.

Among ruins
you can still find the girl in me.
Yes, among castles
you can still find the gypsy in me.
Among turquoise you can still see
the red in me.

Between the *Are you okays?*
I am the *Wonderful, thank you.*
Between the Mondays
I am the upstream fish, the kiss good-bye.
Inside my bones
I am the Milky Way's daughter.

JULIA ALTER-CANVIN

Story of the Conodont and the Noctiluca

Love, can you feel the Kuroshio current moving again,
all those underswirls and bobbins lilting their greyblue toward teal?
The warmswept wash of the Westerlies tells me it is time.
Brackish water blown aside, and nothing but pearls rising to the surface.
Flowmeter registers one thousand and three.

Acropora blooming in the gills of my heart, this is the wave period, Love,
where lagoons become rivers, become lagos, become bay estuaries.
Paddle through this slough with me, the egret's body the only
exclamation mark we need. Remember the call, the cry, the voice
of white wings waving evening in around us.

This, the approach of night, reminds me of our bathymetry,
how the spongeweed lets go her aubergine circles,
how the wrack and the dugong begin their dark, low songs,
and you, Love, my conodont, my mangrove, the starboard cupping
every yellow curve of lancet and latitude.

Swimming through night, I remember you holding me
weightless above you, the Oyashio current pulling softly east and south.
Love, hold me here awhile in the Noctiluca, in the salinity.
There are times when the body makes itself known
by luminescence only, all that foreshore, all those sea lilies opening at once.

The Night Eaters

I like the ones who wait
until everyone else
has gone to bed.
These people, making
peanut butter sandwiches
in the dark, something
my three-square-meals grandma
would never do.

I love their slow chewing
through wheat bread,
the squish of banana,
the stuck jaw of peanut butter.
I love their fierce swallowing
how they flap the crumbs
when footsteps echo down the hall.

I love the half-and-half
drunk straight from the carton.
I love their stretchy robes,
their worn red slippers,
sleepshirts pulled taut
over hips and stomachs.

I love the night eaters.
Apple-pie-at-midnight people.
Licking-honey-from-their-fingertips eaters.
What-will-I-eat-tomorrow? eaters.
Leftover-lasagna-cold-at-one-a.m. eaters.

These are my people, this tribe
making their separate ways
to different kitchens,
down unlit hallways,
following every dark hunger.

JULIA ALTER-CANVIN

What Hums Inside

Sometimes I feel all motor, cylinder and piston—
gearshift arms and windshield eyes—all highway,
asphalt and alloy wheel.

> I want to stop, fall back into a field of lavender,
> or be a footprint sinking into earth right here
> on the path, to slip back slow into the ruby world,
> still enough to feel the thrum of wings.

Life is made of too many Mondays and three o'clocks
and Septembers, when the day wants to tell you
only sunlight, only broken cloud. I've come so close
to roadness, cementness—I can't tell the sound
of motorcycles from a family of bees.

> I want to remember what walking is, to know
> what a weed thinks, just reaching up, stretching toward.
> Only dandelion, only fragment, just this hand
> pulling the apple from the tree. To hear the Queen
> buzzing her commands in nectared syllables.

Some days I am sixty-six-going-on-seventy miles and counting
a thousand rpms, three hundred horsepower, two zillion
milligrams, a hundred trillion cells making up this body. I am this
many words closer to being a better person, this much closer
to the heart of the hive, no more fuel injection or throttle—still
enough to hear the hum of the bee's dream,
quiet enough to hear my own.

On a White-Orange Morning Like This

A cinnamon roll rises over distant hills.
His kiss is yeasty fresh from the oven of sleep
and I wake hungry, yes, I'm hungry
and new blackbirds are nibbling at the sun.

He puts the baby in my body, we play house
and wife and breakfast in bed. He puts the baby
to my breast, she smells like cinnamon bark
and fresh-sprung clover.

These days, morning is a fresh-cut orange,
peel and seed and juice. And he is juice
this morning, I sip his voice tongue by tongue
I drink the Florida of him down.

Yes, today becomes a baby and we hold her
tight with mother-father arms. A kiss pressed
into cheekflesh, a kiss brought from both sides
and fresh rolls from the mistress of pastries.

We are split and buttered, our lips shining,
milk-kissed and freshly-flowered. This is day now
with a hummingbird at my breast
and my husband eats hibiscus by the mouthful.

This is the oven.
This is the graze-bright, grass-grown hill.
This is not a dream of juice.
There are oranges filling every open palm.

The Gift

I was born
able to lift a gate latch
without a sound
and slip into the woods,

to follow creek beds
to crawdads, tadpoles,
dragonflies, and painted ladies,

to ride my bike up a mountain
of moss, milkweed and eucalyptus,

to lie on the grass
in a snow of apricot blossoms,
become
cumulocirrus,

to shelter snails and sow bugs
under the lid of my desk in school,

to make friends with the ants,
build a house
no one could break into—

no chores, no scoldings, no bullies to beat me.

Even in a room full of people,
if I suddenly found I was naked,
I could fade into a slight current of air
or a call of the mourning dove—
no one would bother to notice.

I was born
able to shinny down a rope
into a well. Such comforting
darkness.

Then the long climb upward.

Fallen Crown

One day a crown falls out of nowhere,
lands on my head
and kills me outright. When I
get up again,
I dust off my clothes,
take the crown off and look it over.

It bears six stars
and is inscribed
with Maxwell's four equations
for electromagnetism. While this crown
is not invisible,
you do have to squint
to see it.

It isn't really mine, just came to me
by accident. I usually leave it off,
don't want people staring,
asking lots of questions
or trying to take it from me.

The best thing is
the built-in hearing aid. When I
listen to the story
of any woman, any man
I can just catch sight of their
almost invisible crown.

Questions about Mangoes

The current theological debate is all about mangoes: Are we saved
by our virtue, our faith, or by the limitless grace of mangoes?

Is this the right planet? some ask. I am scraping my teeth
across the pit again to extract another drop from this mango.

The fruit of the Tree of Knowledge is a gift from God.
I know Eden through the sweet flesh of the mango.

Oh help me—they are shaped like a woman's breast.
I am never free in the presence of mangoes.

I am not afraid of the night. I am afraid
of running out of mangoes.

Len is forever in debt to the man, woman
or child who picked this very mango.

A Note on the Use of Metaphor

In the living room, perched
on the curtain rod above the open french door,
is a female house sparrow. It is stunned
by the alien landscape
it has chanced onto
and the impenetrable
patch of clear glass sky
it has now flown into
three times. It glances here,
then there, perhaps feeling
for a moment its own end
rising in its throat. My wife pleads
with it, explains how
to fly down and out, then laments
that her words cannot speak
to its tiny body. At last, we drape
sheets over two wide brooms to form
tall gods and approach the bird,
these majestic beings looming above us,
until it flutters, turns down,
darts out into the spring air.

Invented by the Night

The stork and I were born from the soft mud.
The fullness first was entirely empty.
Light came
without thinking, from a rip in the dark,
the void above and the void below
from a crease in the once-whole void.

Every time I speak
I begin by listening.
The shrew mole
never asked to be born,
nor the potato bug
who finds her mate so beautiful.
I suppose it never was
easy,
but we owe so much
to what is done without hands or eyes.

I live for the day,
yet the day
and I
were invented
by the night.

The Road to Jerusalem

The sacrifice of the goat-king fell into place
As Christ rode into Jerusalem.
The crowd spread their cloaks along the lane.
Oh, how his donkey colt brayed!
Was it his madness that kept him sane?

There are twelve roads into heaven,
But all thirteen lead back again
And vanish in the desert plain.
Some towns are leveled and others in flames.
Only my madness keeps me sane.

So look, the world is beginning again.
We'll need your help to count the slain.
How can we heal a mind rent in twain?
Open your throat, lift up your own soul's refrain
And may its madness make you sane.

Birthday

On this Sunday morning
   she began her sixteenth year
   giving birth to a baby boy
   in the toilet in her cell
   at the county jail.
She is being punished
   for not waiting til
   the nurse came on duty.

On this Sunday morning
   in a coffee bar
   in a little town
   on the California coast
   computer programmers, bright
   in bicycle racing togs
   of many colors, clog in, order
   espressos, ibarras, macchiatos.

These young men began their day
   under warm sun
   speeding through salt air
   blowing in from over Pacific water,
   stretching away
   to lush tropical islands.

A Child's Hand

the day after
bits-of-flesh
were gleaned
from
Bunker Buster
rubble
a
Child's Hand

as perfect
as in life
was found
I am so sorry
little one
it was I
I
the one
who wields
this pen
I cut off
your life
I am so sorry

Iraq, 2003

Grooming

Lured by sunlight,
our two calicos have jumped up
to join us on the window seat.
The cats huddle, groom the glow
of each other's fur with raspy tongues.

We two, aglow with damp-bloom
from our bath, cuddle
under your grandmother's worn quilt,
groom each other
with soft gentle words.

Outside the window, red and green and blue
hues of childrens' kites bob and weave,
bob and weave.
The phone rings.
The cats jump down.

At last, a time and date
for the start of your chemo.
The cats yowl to be let out,
not knowing
how cold the wind.

Cicatrix

She is seated by the window.
He takes the seat beside her.

Tropical islands flow beneath them.
Good vibes flow between them.

After some time has passed,
he speaks in a muffled voice:

Yes. It is painful.
Yes. It's OK to ask
what happened to my face.

After some additional time has passed,
she speaks in a clear voice:

May I see your face
with my fingertips?

Chimes

she brings serenity from the other world
   from which she has so soon come

light soft in from the garden
   glints her mother's girlhood hair
   crescendos my mother's dying light eyes

she leans forward from the breast
   cocks her head
   as would a robin

her tiny bell-voice chimes
   out the names
   she says were given her
   before she became our Sandra

she nestles
   her mother lips to me
   asleep

An Ode to Joy

fills my morning
redwood forest chorus
voices among iris blooms
each fragrant immensity
rocking in its earthen cradle
great boles tower up straight
through a rich greenness of limbs
ever bathed in mists and rains
caressed in lights and winds

A sweep of my eyes startled and stopped
a jade crystalline-brilliance
infant sempervirens   sunrayed-pulsing
Arboreal child   I can not wait for you
through your cyclings of birds
I will go   perhaps to return
find you swept up to intoxicating heights
or gone   desecrated in a massacre
of the splendid   your old earthen cradle
a wound   crusted over with bituminous scabs
for now   I too cradle rock
my brows   crowned with needled-boughs

The Anonymity of Poets

If we had anything at all worth saying,
wouldn't someone be listening? Wouldn't more than the few
straggled round the beaten lectern, eyes closed,
strands of words teasing the heart as Medusa's wild hair,
full of snakes—the venom of meaning, love's poisonous bite—
wouldn't someone stand up, make a motion, a second, say
if not for this, we would have no heart!

How the world glistens as a deer
gutted by the side of the road from collision with careening metal,
the poet bending now over the still warm fur, dark pupils open,
the transmission of something sacred, a last rite,
the promise that this is not the end, that the wet nuzzle of nose,
the thick clot of red, the quiet antler will live on, a reincarnation
into word—this love for the world going on and on as lovers
bantering into the night, the hard argument that if all was meant
to be, why is it so hard to grasp, to say much beyond this
oooh & aagh floating inarticulate out of the throat as a soft orgasm
or a death shudder—when the earthquake that is your life
rifles down your many faults and you split in two, trembling.

If this was at all important, this speaking, somehow essential
to the world going on and on as it does, wouldn't the stadiums
fill at night, the therapists write new books claiming to have found
their language at last, a grammar to shake politics down
to the root, to infuse economists with the lyricism embedded
in numbers, shake the ennui from advertisers' brain stems,
wouldn't the army brass sing a new anthem, everyone pledge
a new allegiance to what lies inside? Tell me, is it worth saying,
is any of this worth saying—words flapping like fish in rarefied air,
waiting to be thrown back into the dark waters from whence
we come, though the world is hungry—and we,
fishers of the deep, with only this thin thread, a hook,
and one wriggling worm.

The Meaning of Life

He is young,
a college student with reddish brown hair,
glasses, pimples, nerdy—slummy olive green sweatshirt
with Santa Cruz skateboard logo, short pants.
The old Java House is almost empty when it happens,
odd assortment of bad rappish punk finally quiet, the café still.
He gets up from a table across the room, saunters
over to the piano, lifts the keyboard cover, sits down and says
I'm going to make something up to no one in particular.
At first, some kind of quiet blues or jazz, fingers wandering
across the keys as lovers down a midnight New Orleans backstreet,
then a kind of swelling as though the sea were brooding & restless,
looking for a storm. Black keys & white begin to swelter
as though the devil's itchin' to get in, but then rise as an airy flutter
light enough to make caramel & dark honey float.

I am so taken by this dark whimsy that my ears cannot tell
by the tasting whether the world is bitter or sweet.
In the listening, all the dogs in me drop their bones,
their incessant gnawing, lay back and paw the air,
soft underbellies willing to be exposed, to be rubbed, to be taken.
And all the prosecutors in me cease their endless bickering
over life's purpose, whether it is, finally, more good than bad,
and couldn't it have been planned a little better. Because here,
in this music, this strange improvisation, is the sound
I have been looking for all my life, a reconciliation of dark
& light no thought can contain—but can finally feel
in this tickle & tease of funny bone, this melting through groin,
this flutter of heart as a hummingbird pressing nectar
into my open, raised mouth—all this as though God were here,
now, as this pimply-faced prodigy haunting the piano stool,
improvising, lost in music, shoulders hunched & swaying,
giving it all away for free.

Every Wound a Kiss

On the wooden step, my son sits considering his apple.
It is more than I can bear.
He is only five, will never again be this young.
Grief is the red apple succulent in my chest,
Gabriel consuming its pale flesh to the core.
After he rises to play, I pick the remaining seeds
from cracks between the boards, plant them deep
beneath my breastbone. It will take

bushels ripe and red to feed this hunger,
and I will need many trees. Last night in a dream,
the orchard stretched on forever, apples falling
from the sky, every wound a kiss.

Sons are meant to bruise fathers, but who knew
it would be with love?

Sin

The worst part is failing to kiss the ground each morning.
Or the cold pot of resentment stirred and simmered
well into the evening. Everything else comes from this,
grows.

It wouldn't be so bad if such immense portions
of good fortune weren't squandered each hour,
minutes the long dead would ransom eternity to regain.

Even now, ripe apples lie rotting casually about the floor,
single bites taken from each—there is
no worm, no snake . . .

only this failure to praise.

A Rose, a Thorn

Watching *Shakespeare In Love* with my daughter, about love,
its betrayal, and how does one explain. Passion's vagaries:
the wilted rose, the bruised fruit—in its season, the bloom,
the blush. Much remains the same,

as in old England's time: whole continents shifting
in the small space of the heart. A single glance or brush
of fingertip, then as now, wilts the body with heat,
the white heat of electrical storm, the distance between
heaven & earth shortened to the length of a breath, a lip.
But can she comprehend,

vaster than the Atlantic's wide basin, the distance between
the woman she may become & the women who first stepped
on these shores? After a few years: wedding bells sounding
as the dull clank about a cow's neck, the fine sheen of young
skin burnished stiff as furniture, a life chosen by father,
by husband. Only later,

across a vast continent of kitchen tables, legs trembling
from tremors rippling beneath every foundation, one woman
after another pushing back her chair, peering into the eyes
of the man across that table, taking what was hers. A rose,
a basket of fruit: to *be* the gardener, the one who clips the stem,
offers the petal & the thorn, the one who sucks the juice
from the pulp down to the marrow of seed. This

gift my daughter ponders, as the movie credits slip across
the screen as a stream of years, not so far removed from this
Shakespearean stage where the only players were men—pretending
the cry of birth, the lament of death, every sound between.
Nothing shields her from what is hers: this prick of thorn,
her petal bruised, this tangle of root growing
beneath secret ground—and in its season,
her blush, her bloom.

How to Know God

Pull up a chair and offer Her a beer,
no come-ons, everyone's always wanting something;
just sit and be silent a while. Good talk comes slow.
Ask how long it's been since someone
patted Her on the back, or even knew
She's generally a Woman. Offer a few
encouraging words, that it's tough being
in charge of such a raucous brood as humanity.
Don't speak too quickly about your own
petty needs & desires, that will come later,
and She'll be happy to listen, then, to each one.
Order a second round, pay for them both;
it's all Her money anyway, but She won't mind—
that's what She made it for. Describe what it's like
where you live, how things shake down here
on the front lines, the advantages and disadvantages
of the cosmic trickle-down effect, how bad things
sometimes happen to good people & vice versa,
but how it's all still really beautiful and pretty amazing
that it works out as often as it does. She might be
impressed at your poise & general good will,
even think language wasn't such a bad invention after all,
what with the weird come-ons & prayers for bizarre things
She entertains everyday. Rising from the corner chair,
She may even give you Her number, but don't come right out
and ask—see if you're chosen. It could be the beginning
of a meaningful relationship, both of you on the lookout
for something that will last past the honeymoon's glow
into the long stretch of unknown road ahead.

Would You Recognize the Truth If You Saw It

A small boy with blue glasses pokes his head
round the corner of the black metal newspaper stand, stares.
I crack the smallest of smiles, enough to send him giggling
for cover—till he reappears inside the empty black cage,
pokes his head through, stares at me again. This time,
I look him full in the face, radiate what gave us birth
those eons ago, this ecstatic recognition of being,
the surprise of it all. Gazing back through oval lenses,
never blinking, he radiates back as though it were still,
all of it, just beginning, as though there were endless time
to love your life this much.

Becoming a Poem

One can take poems anywhere—
stuff the pockets of jeans, the one over the heart—
carry them as love letters or food,
words dug from the ground as potatoes,
feeding off each one.

One can gather poems from anywhere,
for everywhere there is a poem, waiting—
in the broken father's sad slouch,
the child sliding wet from the womb,
the gloss of war before it comes—
everything rare and breathless
when seen from the inside.

One becomes a poem anywhere,
standing in oxfords or thongs, boots
or bare feet—the body a pyre for the burning
that comes in making everything sacred:
the square of office cubes, the tin of factories,
the fields of blood, the profane burned
with a word into our eyes until holy.

Saved

I see it when I prepare food.
Chopping vegetables or pouring out grains of rice
I see how I watch the pieces that get left out
or the grains that fall away from the pot.
I always pick them up.
Taking the extra effort to wash them again
if they've landed on the floor or the counter top,
I put them back in the pan or the soup.
And always I think of the biblical story:
The great Lord God talking
about who will live and who will die
in Sodom and Gomorrah.
Abraham asks, "If I can find fifty righteous people,
will you destroy the whole city?"
Then finally coming down to
"What about one good person—
will you destroy the whole place if I can find one good soul?"

I always think of that and save the grain of rice.
Saying this one has come so far, grown with all the others,
come finally to my kitchen, in my hand,
and now I have dropped it. So I rescue the one grain or bean.

Thinking always if someone saw me,
I would also be rescued.

When I am reminded
who I truly am—
        I am the cook.
        I am the water.
        I am the pot.
        I am the bean
        finally seen and savored.

One Morning on Earth

Ruby-capped finches dart and twitter
through the jasmine bramble
o lark o swallow o hawk
o soul of myself here arrived again
on a morning in April
a morning of dew and pollen and shine
a morning of infinitesimal, abundant perfection
Does the golden stamen of the calla
wrapped in her round white robe know
she will be rumbled by a bumblebee at nine
fluttered by a swallow tail at noon?
Heedless, wanton glory—
so outright, so one-pointed
up from fine shoots pulsing through the earth—
to come to this, before my early morning eyes
my beauty-holding heart
o birds o trees o lilac bushes   yes

From the Castle at Montegufoni, Tuscany

Angles of light cast over
this swatch of ochre earth,
across boxy boulders of soil
carved open by teams of oxen and men.
What sprouts here—aside from olives, aside from
grapes and apples and pears—the poet soul.
Even a barren heart could green here.
Eventually words have to burst out.
One morning, sometime, finally
the teat of this hilly mother
produces another Petrarch,
another Dante, or a girl like Elizabeth
forswears her love
in fourteen perfect lines.

Puccini Square, Lucca

When I am dead will they make a museum around my bones?
My dishes and my cups? Say "These are the pencils
She used." And will they become a famous brand?

Will the streets I walked be revered in a hundred years?
Say "This handkerchief caught her precious tears."
Will schoolgirls want to have a sad-eyed look
Like me because it has come into fashion?

Let others tour this landmark home of genius.
I'll sit out on his curved stone bench in the late light.
I don't really care about Puccini's living room.
Don't need to see his leather books or velvet chair.
Nor sit at the family desk where notes
First poured from his slender fingers.

I care about what is the same in him and in me.
And I care how much it has not changed—
That a soul lives and creates from an instant,
The lilt of trees along the Piazza,
A girl wrapping her cloak against a dark sky.

I care how grace visits.
The inner sound that tumbles out.
That sudden rush when it begins.
What told him and what tells me—
Now is the moment. Take up your pen.

Still Life on the #5, Amsterdam

Last seats near the back door,
mother and boy of about four.
We stand above them, holding the poles
as the crowded tram swerves
and shuttles around corners
just inches from the other cars.

He gives her the core of a green apple.
She holds it gracefully by the stem,
no sticky juice on her fingers.

He is tired. She croons to him in mother-tongue.
He draws his little legs up and turns his body 'round.
She moves her parcels further out on her legs.
On her lap he lays his bright head down.

Her left hand holds the apple core.
The right one smoothes his hair,
his shirt, warms over his legs,
rounds his bottom,
rests on his back.

Sun blazes across this mother and child
in the sudden way of Amsterdam light.
The fine hairs on her neck shine.
Golden skin glows.
Stillness and contentment radiate
from the back of her bowed neck.

JENNY D'ANGELO

Magnetics of the Heart

You can rub your chest in the hot sun.
Regret nothing in your afternoons.
Make a refuge for the trembling heart.

You can smell the violets, smell the lilacs,
let the crimson roses capture you.
Feel your grateful heart.

Once I filled my rooms with folded cranes
and prayer flags, lit incense and white candles,
all my house a glowing hearth.

Cherries in a crystal bowl, stems sticking out
like thin arms, connected
to a plump, sweet heart.

Scrub jays, juncos, red-topped acorn woodpeckers
eat from the Queen's bounty—
her outstretched heart.

Leather bound books with titles in gold,
paperbacks with crinkled spines, thin or fat,
the volumes of a well-read heart.

Light in bright foliage,
rainbows through edges of beveled glass,
the catchings of a lightened heart.

Four chambers, right and left,
auricle and ventricle; undivided against itself,
this makes a cheerful heart.

A heart-shaped bone remains atop
the glowing funeral pyre. The angels say
not even death can end the numinous heart.

To My Community of Poets

Blessings on you,
my sprawling band of leaders,
sometime stragglers,
and glorious, wise late-bloomers;
you with pencils poised,
notebooks open, scraps of paper ready;
you with ink-stained pockets, knapsacks full,
you in your coffeehouses and your studios, all hail!

Blessings on your eyes
keen to find poems on cracker boxes,
mangoes in the morning, or a pigeon's twirling strut.
When other folks are watching NASCAR, how you write!

Blessings on your insight—
sitting in circles at solstice
you enter the temple of silence,
hear the confetti of birds, let the light reach you.
Then write as turquoise and claret
splash through your hearts.

Blessings on your greetings,
arms up in the air like a shot of hope.
On a rain-dark day when the world is logged with doubt,
when promises lie spent in the mouths of false leaders
and sound bites dull our ears,
then the daily ritual of rising seems a thankless thing.
You find the words hidden under stones or behind locked doors.
With your caps full of stars you show reasons to continue.
You magnify small kindnesses, warm as a red wool jacket,
turn a cold ache into a pail of sunshine,
a charm of finches bursting out.

O blessed rowdy, rough-handed workers of word magic.
O beloved friends, happy and foolish. O relentless believers:
there is no wrong way to write a poem
and fifty million ways to do it right.

If I Were to Dream a Poem

If I were to dream a poem
She would be you love

Dark as crimes at night
black as the prosecutor guarding my soul
you, who promise delight in the morning
rising like birdsong between river and sea
over houses full of care and pain
and beneath humming wires

If I were to dream a poem
She would be you love

Light as ripe wheat fields
white as a child's first communion
you, who fulfill yearning through the day
descending like dusk between desert and plain
into this home of warmth and ease
beneath star filling sky

If I were to dream a poem
She would be you love

always with me
even amid wreckage
and in my forgetting and foolishness

When Mother Died

When mother died
I felt her presence all around.

I dream of her at times.
She still lives in those dreams
part memory, part unbroken connection
to mother love.

She taught me to love
Mary, as my perfect mother
mother Mary, maiden Mary
divine vessel broken and made whole.

Now, after so much living
Mary still comes to me
spirit of the sea, the morning star.
Gaia swirled in blue and white.

August 2006

When I Get Mine
For Mom

When I was ten,
I ate the best
piece of fruit
of my life.
With care,
I dug a hole
and planted that pit
in our backyard.

How the family laughed!
They swore,
Nothing'll grow.
When a sapling sprouted,
they shook their heads
and warned, *Well,
it won't bear fruit,
you know.*

Now Mom lives
in that house alone
and every summer
she has more nectarines
than she can eat,
more than she can
give away.

When I get mine
we shake our heads
and laugh
sweet juice
running down
our chins.

Cicatrices

I am a tree the sky is stretching
A fixed point in an endless
Circling of ghost-clouds, sun and moon
So lonely, I know I'm not alone

I am a beckoning of leaves,
Radiant faces, riotous tongues
Set loose by a chaotic storm
O inconsolable wind, sing me
Sights I'll never see but falling bark
Becomes loam between silver stones
Home for this creaking torso
Of streaming tears

Although the fiery flash at night
Lashes a black scar, still my skin
Burnished by the rain, does shine and shine
What does it matter if the song sung
Is starlight or morning's boisterous bird-scolding?
Even as the body shivers, the spirit dances

Intertidal Zone

Love, your touch is a tropical current streaming
through my once, stone-still body of cold water.

Before you, I dreamt the dogfish shark conspired
with the gorgeous medusas, their venomous tentacles

pinching off pieces of the heart I thought could not grow back.
Those were the long, ink-black nights of my past, when lost in thickets

of swaying kelp, I choked upon their brine-filled goblets, wanting only
to renounce this dangerous longing. But dawn's dark-bellied storm clouds

have retreated, below the waking life returns unstained. Even yesterday's
silver gauze of rain abates. The sun blazes upon the water's up-turned face

and a sudden florescence flashes in my stark depths! Your balmy breath
upon my neck adorns the ocean floor with emeralds and pearls—sea lettuce,

fine bits of shell. Your whispered words coax the iridescent sea creatures
from their secret grottoes, feathery white antennae trembling in the drift and
       flow.

As your fingertips trace the sheltered coves of my body's hidden terrain,
underwater flowers unfurl, sweep the rocks with silken moss. Colonies of
       dahlia

and jewel anemones bloom. Their fuchsia, burnt-burgundy and absinthe
       tentacles beckon,
beguile, then soundlessly swallow prey. Love, our desire is a complex mingling
       of tides,

temperatures, and topographies—life shimmering beneath the riotous swell.
Sinking deeper, we find our exhaled bubbles whirl upwards, turn to light.

———
After an article by Jennifer S. Holland, "Beneath the Irish Isles," *National Geographic,*
March 2005.

Chaos Reigns

Earth laughs in flowers
—Ralph Waldo Emerson

Morning's garden whirs with the rambunctious bumblebees,
Pollen-coated and plummeting orbs, how they appall
The ladybugs, dainty on foxgloves' velvet leaves.
Oh, the tiger lily stamens do tremble and call!

Pollen-coated and plummeting orbs, how they appall
The johnny-jump-ups, forget-me-nots, and proper hollyhocks.
Oh, the tiger lily stamens do tremble and call!
While those rollicking bees shimmy and shake the flowering stalks.

The johnny-jump-ups, forget-me-nots, and proper hollyhocks
Sigh in unison with the sunflowers' sultry sun-scents.
While those rollicking bees shimmy and shake the flowering stalks,
Blossom-centers beckon and summon like billowing tents.

Sighing in unison are the sunflowers' sultry sun-scents,
Lion-mane shadows are cast across the clinging sweet peas.
Blossom-centers beckon and summon like billowing tents,
For all the world's mesmerized by a game of taunt and tease.

Lion-mane shadows are cast across the clinging sweet peas,
And the ladybugs, dainty on foxgloves' velvet leaves.
For all the world's mesmerized by a game of taunt and tease,
Morning's garden whirs with the rambunctious bumblebees.

Unrequited

Love, I remember stooping to kiss the goose on its glossy
beak, how I got my nose pecked, a strawberry bruise
I treasured for weeks. Drawing back, quick as a gasp,

   I was chased away from the water—my first love

spurned at seven by the bird I thought would be mine. Do I
waste my time trying to learn how to watch from a distance,
sidle up slowly, feed my desire in equal

   measure with reason? Years later, the mirror makes plain

the skinny neck I stretch against danger, while it's too late
for these eyes, like two black seeds, already planted deep
in their wanting. My feathers ruffled, I flap my wings, squawk,

   "Kiss me! Kiss me, fool and I won't bite you back!" Love,

you teach me not to be meek, nor too mild-hearted, this girl
who learned to live with the goose's lesson, who ran
to the lake's hard edge, arms flung wide, lips puckered.

In These Five Remaining Days
After Hafez

In these five remaining days, I see
I've spent my life bellowing like a mule,
feeling broken beneath a burden
that was mine to learn to carry
or the weight of another's I could not ease.

In these four remaining days, the robe
that has been my body, revels in
its own unraveling. Inside, a hummingbird
hovers, half-inside a flower, then
zips away, stitching the sky with iridescence.

In these three remaining days, I am still,
knowing what ripens below, soon breaks
through the duff, finds some light—
a rose-colored mushroom, quietly
glistens in the redwood mist.

On this, the second to last day, I ride
a riptide out to sea, find myself
fixed again to the ocean's umbilicus.
Rocked upon her heaving breast, I taste
the briny tears we share, let go my thirst.

Oh this, my final day of living,
with every last breath, I make a plea
for the chance to hold aloft a hundred
more burdens, a friendship to sip, a forest
to sit in, singing thank you, thank you, thank you!

ROBIN LYSNE

Bear Nights and Sterling Moons

Before I met you my fields were wide and flat,
        I wandered around for days screaming and
    singing my pain to the corn fields.

You first opened to me when you said,
        "It is my left side where I hold my grief, too."
    Then I to you, "I see a bear and a buffalo, white as snow."

You said nothing,
        opened your clenched fist to two fetishes
    —a bear and a buffalo—carved of white stone.

You fill me with your darkness from behind the stars.

We play in redwood forests,
        mountains thick with caves to hide in
    and waterfalls in which to bathe.

You bring me shade and more rain.

We have seen green iguanas in Puerto Rico,
        blue waters of Salvador Bahia
    and the falls of Iguazu.

We have traveled through the loss of our daughter,
        joys of our two sons
    and near death of one.

Oh you fill me with the darkness of underwater caves,
        swimming through beds of kelp,
    in ten thousand leagues of learning.

You remind me   water teaches evaporation,
        darkness is a silent relief,
    the noon sun hides your shadow.

I remind you   each of us chooses
            the buffalo plains—to live each day
        or bear caves—to take one more breath.

I feel all that has passed.
            You let it go.
        We climb together and   alone.

Beyond our wildest buffalo dreams   we fly.
            Filled with bear nights
        and sterling moons   we rest.

Filled with turquoise oceans   we dive.
            Into red canyons and
        through ochre plains   we run.

Oh those peaks beyond peaks
            and always through
        the darkness between the stars   we dance.

At the end of each day
            we come together
        and rest in each other's arms   sublime.

Prow to Bow

Silky rattlesnake grass, hulls
shake into my hand.
Tiny boats
cup into each other,
their seeds tucked
into the prow.

Summer heat dries them,
wind shakes loose
these tiny vessels
to sail into unknown harbors.

Some fall into deep grass,
others sink in wooded glens,
still others sail down
unmarked streams
to chart their passage home.

Raspberry

Red nugget
tiny sacks of sweet juice
cotton stalk
you are full summer swollen
I pluck then pop you
between my ready puckered lips
roll you between
tongue and roof of mouth
burst of joy

Roots and Rice

Father, how we have smoothed that black stone passed between us,
   the years of polishing water mixed with sand.

Is this the last dance we take around our ancestral tree? As we move,
   I perceive how deep the root of you is in me.

Branches sprout from my head, blossoming now
   from your not-so-gentle pruning.

Yet your white bird dreams have taken flight through your daughters,
   while grandchildren live their wildest crow careening.

This ancient conflict we've maintained: Science as the way for you,
   the dark silence of the pond for me,

Still you want to pound me with your measuring stone,
   yet the flour of this self is made for poems,

Besides, we have come to the end of pricing
   and dividing these grains of rice.

There is nothing more to say,
   just one last long walk through this winter garden.

Two old fools arm in arm, circling around a black bowl of white rice,
   who laugh and spin again this ancient sign of wholeness.

Pacheco Pass

Reins of wires loop
across golden hills
to water dammed, surging,
funneled to rotating turbines.

Our Ford truck moves westward
towards another source,
sun setting beyond felted hills
lined with furrows of trees,
folded dales where rivulets flow
into the San Luis Reservoir.

We cross the dam, a four-lane highway.
On the left, acres of water.
On the right, steep hills hide us
cool in long shadows,
now blazing sun,
now shade again.

Horses cluster among shadows,
those long tree shapes under trees
that spot the hillsides with dark green leaves,
dark gray stretching
longer, longer,
blending with each other,

joining the east side of the hill
pulling blue shade across the ridge
blanketing everything in cool darkness
as the sun sinks behind Hollister, Gilroy,
now the Pacific rim of the Monterey Bay.

Honey Strands

It is time to wash
       and braid my hair,
   to sit alone
       and watch the bees.
To hive within myself,
         taste honey.

Now is the time for weaving,
      for gathering sweetness
   humming golden fiber
         into my being.

It is time to compose
      my internal fabric.
To begin my tapestry
      from what has fallen
        to the floor.

Corner of Montana and 15th

Santa Monica, 3/6/03

A tanned man with a muscular frame that is softening, aging ex-
body builder talks to a man with a leather coat worn enough to
have character standing next to his motorcycle about what percent
of the population is in prison, how oil will pay for the Iraqi
invasion, how arrogant, crazy the Bush administration, an exact
conversation I heard in Santa Cruz the other day as if their words
displaced here now like birds that have migrated south outside the
parking lot of Wild Oats Market across the street from Cal Fed
Bank a black security guard pacing its perimeter like a caged animal
singing clips of songs under his breath or is it poem lyrics kitty
corner from Spec Tech latest in eyewear fashion against a backdrop
of cars braking, stopping, turning left a girl in sweatpants walking
an oversize white poodle, pigeons circling the base of a tree with
new leaves budding that fresh green that doesn't know itself yet
and pointed spores hanging like Christmas tree ornaments or stars
or smart bombs and how one quarter of the world's incarcerated
are in prison in the United States—it's big business—more than in
Russia and China combined two women waiting at the bus stop
with rolled yoga mats until the bus comes, pulls over, eats them
alive a sprinkling of pedestrians, young mother pushing a stroller
then two minutes later, another, two children carrying sweaters,
backpacks, school must be out a gentle breeze blowing off the
coast on this sunny day just a cloud or two the perfect kind like in
the story books any hint of smog completely washed away and I
swear it is the most beautiful perfect blue sky I have ever seen here
on this day of March 2003, even with all of us held hostage for
weeks now, suspended on the knife blade of a war threat hoping no
one gets sliced the two men enumerate all the crimes of Bush and
Cheney and that witch Condoleeza Rice (not all Blacks are cool like
you think, man) but the most shocking thing is a woman who walks
by, homeless, mumbling, her hair a wild spray of gray her skin
sunburned already in-not-yet spring and when she looks at me I see
she has fungus growing on her face, rimming her eyebrows, its
brown and black texture riding roughshod over her cheeks,

coursing up her neck, shadowing her jaw, as if she is becoming tree, wearing a tattered plaid man's shirt and gray sweatpants so worn at the seams they are split and as she passes I see the back flaps open then close with each step, reveal a wedge of naked buttocks and I see now the edge of the pants are stained brown she must be seventy or seventy-five years old and of all the homeless I've seen this one still has the capacity to shock me although everyone else ignores, doesn't even seem to see yet she has enough presence of mind to turn back ask me, do you have a dollar how can she ask for a dollar and not see the mold growing on the back of her hands? I reply like I always do to the homeless not today sorry not today I watch as she turns away and I think has mother earth herself risen up to ask me for a dollar and have I said no? Is this what she looks like these days? Always my generosity comes dripping later in guilt form, hobbling behind, crippled by my fear, my lack of action, my perpetual no to every situation as the two men beside me close out their conversation commenting on the budget for education the fear of every John Doe sitting in his little mortgaged home frightened like rabbits they wave good-bye . . . good-bye . . . good-bye . . . as mother earth disappears up the sidewalk spilling over, almost on fire, such an abundance of sunlight.

One Moon, Two Moons

Our moon, our mother's beaming face leaning close, cradling us.
Their moon, a mother's soothing lined with fear, twice as real.
Our moon a beginning, theirs an end. Ours,
a blessing, theirs, a curse.
Ours, a communion wafer, a golf ball, a Rolex watch.
Theirs, a smart bomb, mine in the sky, bomb crater.
Ours, a baseball. Theirs, a pocked rock.
Ours, pearl pendant suspended
on night sky's breast. Theirs, simple bread.
Ours, a moment of romance.
Theirs, a life of prayer.
Ours, a cue ball sinking the eight ball corner pocket to win, win, win.
Theirs, an eyeball, a skull, an unrecognizable body part.
Theirs, a fortune teller. Ours,
bikinied model from *Sports Illustrated*.
Crystal ball . . . curled fetus.
Their moon, a moan, ours, a howl.
Theirs, a claw, ours, a smart bomb.
Ours, a ball bouncing through night sky's roulette wheel of luck.
Our wins, their losses.
Our cursed blessings. Their blessed curses.
Theirs, a mute moon. Ours, a barking guard dog.
Theirs, wheel of a wagon circling refugees.
Wheels of a sports car, a limousine, a Humvee.
Their moonlight borderless.
Ours, barbed wired.
A dirty bomb.
Whose bomb? Whose moon?
Theirs, last light in darkness.
Ours, satellite dish for global positioning
trapping earth in the bite of its grid,
stillborn and breeding.
Whose womb? Whose moan?
Theirs, parchment of belief,
seed someday sprouting life into a dead sea sky,
soul in hiding.

Home on Leave

He sits on the porch
in an intimate Arkansas dark,
the arc of his childhood flies across:
a shooting star.

He once counted heroes
on baseball cards,
held up jars of fireflies
he'd caught,
his skin lit with the wonder
of their fading.

Back then he reached
into the cloaked dark
like beneath that first girl's skirt,
gingerly explored,
but now, the darkness
has grown teeth,
could bite his tongue off
if he didn't shout out
tough words to ward away evil:
While we have
boots on the ground,
we should kill as many
terrorists as we can.

A dog barks down darkness
from the middle of a field
as his angry words flick from his tongue,
fire, a dragon or a small god speaking
bolts of lightning,
this super hero,
one year out of high school,
sits in the small space
near the hearth, so changed,
as crickets rub their delicate legs together

JOANNA MARTIN

in the distance,
paint the dark
gold
with sound.

Armed with baseball cards
and paper-thin, burnt-out firefly wings,
either way he wins,
comes back a hero if he lives,
a martyr if otherwise.

Proud killer,
dark god,
destroyer,
It's too late now to worry about
whether or not there were weapons
of mass destruction,
and suddenly the Arkansas landscape
is a video game.
Our hero's muscles burst
from beneath his taut skin.
He can't stay in one place,
tramples the woods,
his feet turn the earth beneath him,
a few steps more and he's in Iraq,
firing round after round,
leaving behind a trail of dead crickets,
leaf debris and his own shorn curls.

Spiraling between Good and Evil, Love

Me and my dog sitting here together on the lawn chair in the backyard after turning off the TV—she is a democratic dog, like me, and she, too, is against the war. However, we have decided to try and not think about it for a while. We deliberately notice a cascade of geranium spilling over the planter box towards the light. Wonder which way the weather will decide. Are the clouds coming or going, thinning or gathering? Are the squares of sunlight appearing between them brightening or fading? Lasting longer each time?

We notice the blossoms on the plum tree are gone, the ones on the apple are just now opening and on the avocado, half the blossoms still cling to the branches, half have fallen. We see the trees, for the first time, as music, a recurring refrain replaying each spring: plum . . . avocado . . . apple . . . plum . . . avocado . . . apple . . . or The Three Graces: buttocks . . . breasts . . . buttocks . . . back . . . front . . . back . . . and we can't for the life of us understand why we suddenly feel so elated in this time of deep sorrow, this time of war, reach to the clouds, the blossoms, to explain it, realize in the midst of tears and depression there is still a part of us that has remained intact, that can still lift. Realize our core is a joyous one. See now how beautiful we each are, how deep our love, how good the living. We try and name it, spirit, perhaps, or soul. Dog/Spirit, Human/Soul. Human/Spirit, Dog/Soul. Remember ourselves again.

Lovposuction

I talked to the doctor
I have to stop loving him
Do you have a machine
to take away
each of my cells
that love him?

Yes
It's just delivered
I call it
the Lovposuction Machine

She inserted the tube
She started the pump

And when she was done
all that was left
of where I had been

Were
My peek-a-boo toed dancing shoes
My dress with red roses outlined in beads
My Mickey Mouse watch
My black lace see-through bra
The Greek pendant he kissed
My glasses with their dappled frames
My sparkly rhinestone hair barrette
And my removable bridge
with three teeth

Cement Mixing

Please Love
put your shirt back on

I have spent the last two hours
looking at the small mole
near your tanned backbone

Marveling how broad your shoulders are
in comparison to your waist

Loving the supple changes in your triceps
as you shovel the sand
into the maw of the mixer

And when you turn around
my breath catches
at the beauty of your chest hair
beginning to turn gray

It was all black
when we built the gazebo
in the heat
two years ago

I enjoy the luxuriousness of it
your nipples almost hidden
beneath its generosity

"What?
What was that you said?"
I did not hear it with the effort
of keeping this lusting hand
from bridging the two feet
between us

"Oh! More water?
Right away!"

My eyes feast on how flat your stomach is
with its small navel
Only a discreet rounding
to declare your humanness

Please Sweetheart
I cannot bear
to look one more minute
without touching
more than our usual places
arm
shoulder

My hand remembers
your permitted touching
of your stomach
after reading you
my first love poem "To X"
But it was a covered stomach
then

What did you say?
Was that five scoops of gravel?
"Yes"
I hope I counted right
I wonder how much difference it makes

I did not feel your hair
under your shirt
when I put my ear against your chest
to hear your heartbeat
down in the basement electrifying lamps
but I remembered it was there

Look at you!
Look at you
you torturer!
I think you know it too

What are you asking me?
Are you getting sunburned?
"Yes you are."

Oh
Why did I say it?
Now you are putting on your shirt

I was in pain with my hand's desire
and my promise
not to touch you
But I could have taken it
a little longer

Please
my Darling
take it off again!

Morning Ritual

I search my bed each morning
and find the pericardium
the covering to my heart
where it has slid overnight
out of my chest

I take the shards of my heart
from the sheet and
fit them together
to make the
four parts once more

I fasten the
right atrium to the
right ventricle
the left ventricle to the
left atrium

I join the two halves and
slip my heart
into its sheath
I slide the whole
back into my chest
I connect the
aorta and the
vena cava

Even though I will not see you
I touch the
sino-auricular node
and shock my heart
into beating

Now I know
I have another whole day
to pretend to be alive

Variations on a Certain Theme

My new beau captures my attention in a kiss
as long and wide as a harmonica
with the varied movements of his tongue
to block certain notes
and force out others
in an irregular arpeggio of tones

Now he is holding me between his knees
as though I were a viola d'amore
as he bows me—arco
and plucks me—pizzicato
until we resonate
at the same vibration

He embraces me so tenderly and close
just like an accordion player
squeezing my breath in and out
fingering my keys
ever more deftly
until our melody grows
from piano to forte

Do I hear a drumbeat?
No it is his heart
I listen to it
accelerando
impassionato
Enticing our delight
to ever more irresistible
crescendos

Doors

Let's say the fruit fell before it was ripe
because the season didn't know itself.
Everyone knows we've had an early spring.
I wouldn't be surprised if it's time for a blue moon.

Let's say the atmosphere was thick with understatement
because translation is so difficult.
Everyone knows the mind and heart only put up with one another.
I wouldn't be surprised if they killed each other off somehow—

I wouldn't be surprised if that means freedom.
Everyone knows it's the soul that matters
because nothing else really lasts.
Let's say we're stuck with the invisible thing.

Everyone knows when one world ends, another begins
because our lives are made of doors.
I wouldn't wonder if we never looked back.
Let's say there's nothing to forgive.
Let's say we're sorry.

Yoga

Today the blonde boy revealed himself.
Not in postures or deep yoga breath,
but in tattoos that stretch the length of both arms.

One arm claims the silhouette of a woman
truck-flap style: stand-at-attention nipples,
tight waist, round butt. Her shape ripples

during Downward Dog. On the other arm
a bolder woman sits: hands high above her head,
legs open wide to expose her rose.

Now I am certain that a rose is not a rose
and I am not her. Yet, why does it seem
like my secret splayed all over his arms?

If he thinks he has taken hold of something,
say, sexuality or manhood, remind him
of the rose that brought him into the world.

The rose over which he holds no dominion.

On Neruda

Look how he numbered his poems
as they spilled out over the rim of his life,
currents always heading in the direction
of Mathilde, in whose hair
he saw stars and vines, whose hands
furnished him with prayer,
certain dark things to love. Moments
brimmed with moons, apples, bread, sky.
Like a pomegranate, his heart's center grew
crowded with seeds and stars, which he
sprinkled across his garden
as a way of insisting on beauty,
so that now, his voice pulls me
into the earth's core, to the underneath
of love, which is more love.

Dandelions

1

These days a mother and a father
cannot dwell inside the same poem.

Trees have barely enough time
to lengthen into their shadows.

Always there seems something
worth risking everything for.

2

I recall how late afternoons
my mother slept. She pulled the shades
early, closed her eyes
and entered the fabricated dark.

I know what she was looking for
and that the voices in her head distracted her
from love's increasing silence.

I understand her need to leave the world
and grasp the bed pillow like a lifeboat.
What saves us today may not save us tomorrow.

3

The moment we turn away
the last light bathes the leaf.

The moment we stop listening
the word gets fully defined.

When Van Gogh peered through the gate
he saw a sea of yellow stars
bowing in the wind.

Not dandelions.

Santa Cruz Fall

I was born into the season of death
in the raw, damp month of November
while rain-soaked leaves stuck to the soles
of my mother's shoes.

If she could take back her life, I wonder what
she would undo. The ten pregnancies,
one every other year for nearly
a quarter of her life? The nights my father threw
grandmother's china collection against the wall,
leaving pieces small enough
to diminish the meaning of love?

When I close my eyes,
I am sitting at the top of the stairs,
palms cupped over my ears, humming a song
to drown out the noise.
It's what's in your own mind that saves you.

Tonight acorns fall on the metal roof of my
Santa Cruz house. The sound of rain is amplified
to the beat of one hundred conga drums
reminding me of the menace of our existence.

At least, that is what I remember,
but memory is not much more
than an accumulation of darknesses
against which we must impress a deeper light.

When my son came into the world gasping for air,
I no longer took oxygen for granted.
I learned how to press my mouth against his and blow
until his chest rose and fell like a white balloon.

It's the way beginnings look like endings
that have some of us confused. The way
invitations precede leave-takings
and a smile can indicate good-bye.

And how, some nights, there is no moon.

Small Things

The mourning dove
mourns all day
in the clean towel of the sun.

It loves the sound
of its own loneliness.

This morning I recalled
when I had only to touch you

with my small white hands
to set the world right.

Now I take small things,
for instance

the bend in the brook,
that branch's shadow—

and that's how I rescue
the broken day.

Old pen
Hand cramping up
Wood, cracking in the coldness.

Ω

Non,
interference.
sad engine;
willful robot
sad harbinger
one I take to task.

My engine, my self

Ω

In the oven
            of conflict
Mis-placed desire
Shook up
Humble, learning.

Ω

Against   the sore back
The cushion
of the lawn chair.
A constant red heat.
Vertical bed of Stars.

Carpenter

Ω

A door   without
          a handle
Cold   of midsummer
              night air
Cow   in the distance
Moos   for its lost love

Ω

Ancient raindrops
          you pound down on the rich
              as well as the poor
But that's not quite true
          Rich, in-side houses
          And polling places

          Poor
Outside,
In the rain!

Elections 2 November 2004

Ω

Hawk, Freeway, Absent Trees

The bird
sits on a wire
unaware
of what we took away from him

Ω

Mouth
Curtain of muscle
Air
Chamber with resonance
My-stery of speech

Ω

I found
a strand
of your hair
Slender strong filament
Protein
burning, bright
Web-element
For what
Weaves us.

Ω

Night Poems

1.

She scratches
Her head
Then cleans herself
And paws at the infinite

Cat

2.

Untutored, you sit there on
The textured stucco,
Like me,
Entranced with light

Moth

3.

You came to me   and put   your arms
                 around me, last night
lay, with me and loved me
Deer, deer.

On your way up the hill
With your big rack of horns
Gently brushed me
Deer deer.

Ω

Poem to My Father

I take apart your body
       And I hear this creaking.
Your wood
Tells me it's been tense so long:
I hear this letting go sound
What   can I say?
        I love you, you loom who wove
                me!

Ω

CAROL RODRIGUEZ

Safe

A mother counts her children when an ambulance wails,
ticking off location with absent compulsion.
Melissa—in her room, John—at the neighbor's, but where is Michael?
Hurtling recklessly toward the beach in a buddy's car,
out of reach. Not safe.

When I tell my son later, he scoffs, listing the odds
with impervious disregard, confident in his own immortality.
I persist, attempt to explain
emotion that transcends logic, fear that laces the hem
of every parental love, but he grins
and lopes out the door, the car outside running.

Secretly, a mother believes her children are only safe in her
reach, small hands clasped in hers when they are young,
the strident love of curfews and questions when they are older.
But she knows this is not so, as she sits on the couch
flipping channels, ear tuned for the click of the door,
turns over in bed, exasperated, peering at the digital green glow.

He thinks he should come and go as he pleases, now that
he's older. *Don't you trust me?* my son challenges.
But we both know that's not the point.
I still remember tending to the scraped knee, the homework,
distracted by the sound of my own life roaring in my ears.
I worry it will come back to haunt me,
the escaped tragedy when I wasn't looking.

They are our deepest vulnerability, the knife that hovers over
our hearts. We relinquish their lives into their impatient hands
each morning, watch them catapult out the door.

Every morning, they fling it high into the air, a wide banner,
let it stream out behind them, fearlessly, joyously.
Every morning, we watch,
terrified and proud.

Confessions of '96

Carol pulls open another book,
fingers the pages of another possibility,
slides another young man down her life
and whispers, *now* . . . and *now*. . . .

The best poems are sometimes the ones never written,
existing only as sensation that glimmers in the air,
steams the senses like rain on summer-hot asphalt.

She could've turned away from them,
the ones who caught her scent and smiled.
She could've said, *no* . . . and *no*. . . .

But we know what's inside of us, don't we?
Even if we could've lived a million lifetimes
without facing that certain truth.
We know we love chocolate.
We know we can't help slicing the sky,
even when it falls to pieces around us.

Carol keeps her young men around her
like slippers, trying them on for size,
not sure if she's Cinderella
or the Prince.

Nine

I am nine and small enough still
to pick a palm tree from the irrigated row
along the desert road, slip between the dried
palm fronds, drawn down like sheltering wings,
into the calm, close space, harboring lizards,
rattlesnakes and sometimes,
barefoot explorers.

The light is cool and stained-glass green
in the accordion-pleated cocoon and I flop down
on my belly, legs flipped up to fit the narrow space.
Just enough filtered light to read,
I chew bitten-down nails, turn another page.

I can hear my mother calling out the kitchen door,
can almost hear the clatter of pots, the refrigerator
opening, closing with a thud.
Dinner soon, but still time left to read.

I am the girl in the book. She reads on a stoop
in Brooklyn, half a candy bar saved beside her.
She has a charming wastrel of a father, a sickly brother
and a plucky mother. We are as different as night and day.
We are the same.

Bicycle tires crunch on the road outside, my little brother's
tuneless hum wafting in and water drips a small pool
from the irrigation pipe at my elbow.
A cricket keens nearby.

My mother calls again, impatience lifting her voice.
One more call before my father's whistle means business.
I finish the chapter, dog-ear my page and sit up,
brushing damp sand from my legs and forearms.

Outside the secret tent of palm fronds
is the late, pale blaze of summer evening,
my sister's sandals slapping down the street,
the click of the gate, dinner.
I crouch inside still, weighing seconds
like tiny insects, a hum of solitude.

The light is cool and stained-glass green
and I hear my mother calling.

Pyromania

When he was a boy, my ex-husband used to start fires.
Fascinated with the science of combustion, puzzling
the time it took the thin ribbon of gasoline to wolf a lit match,
he set the field behind his house ablaze
and his mother, fetched from work, beat him
with the pointy heel of her pump all the way home,
furious and hobbling.

While married, our small house baked
with his leftover devotion, as he stoked the small stove
at its center, feeding the only thing left
still greedy for his attention,
while I slunk into the cool of the back rooms,
surreptitiously cracking windows.

Now he lives with a woman who fans his flame
and they dip and curl in eternal ignition,
while I stand at the flung-open door,
swallowing up darkness in cold, giant gulps,
the crackle of night rushing into me.

Our Mother's Legacy

We practice our mourning in cars,
my brothers, my sisters and I,
pillowed in lives too rushed for grief,
reaching, each of us, for the only moments left
when the window opens and the sharpest images
slip into place, ordinary memories
her face . . . that dress. . . .
So crisp they challenge the truth of air,
the trees in their reincarnated raiment
blowing by,
the sun.

We follow each other like birds heading south,
each in cars that swoop in and out of traffic,
the year of loss sending us into living rooms
weighed down in sorrow,
cemeteries, grey with rain and fog.
Our talisman becomes the recognized bumper,
the familiar silhouettes through the back window
as we weave through lanes as if they were
effortless sky.

We practice our mourning together,
my brothers, my sisters and I,
each a voice that remembers, a hand at
the nape of our necks, the mother father touch
that echoes in our eyes,
lifts us from our pillows every morning
and filters into dreams every night.

It becomes the gold thread that binds us,
stitches our hearts together,
a love that aches in unison and
breathes out solace.

The Walt Within

They weren't all like Walt, you know,
striding across the countryside with his
duffle and pipe, battered hat pulled low
at a jaunty angle to block the sun.

They mostly had jobs,
my old mentors—Pablo, Wallace,
William Carlos and Mary—
paying to Caesar from one hand
while the other dropped coins of
dusky delicacy
onto crisp, white paper.

This is what I tell myself
as I sit at my desk, data spilling
into the fluorescent hum of the room,
while my barbaric yawp surges out
the screened window, winging its way
over concrete and butterflies, over
dark crumbling soil,
into the bellowing chorus
of the world.

JOAN SAFAJEK

At the High Tide Line

Ants shine black
in morning sun,
big on dry sand.
Over leaves,
around pebbles,
along separate paths,
they hurry, hurry,
hurry. One carries a bit
of sun-bleached claw.
Many dead crabs.
I don't know why.
Names on cliffs above
carved into sandstone.
Travis loves Sarah.
Esther Marie, 2003.
Jarret. Jody.
Irrepressible,
this impulse to trace,
if only a name,
in time.
I break apart
a fresh claw,
the flesh
offered to ants
who change course
to avoid it,
diligent
in their search
for something else.

On Our First Anniversary at Sphinx Lake

We walk for days
up river and steep
side canyons
past the massive
stone sphinx to reach
an alpine meadow
where we make love
naked in August sun
by a small stream
among columbine
and purple shooting stars
that grow up out of wet
tundra. Looking down
into my eyes
you do not see
curve of glacial basin
peaks above
and all around us.
Already I know
you wish to leave
the marriage.

I don't want to vanish
into pleasure. I keep
my eyes open wide
and when we cum
together, with almost
unbearable concentration,
I look out
into empty sky
and place our joy
in that blue
granite silence
forever.

In Memoriam

I hold the letter
my sister-in-law sends
and cry for the family
I lost to divorce,
my mother-in-law
now ninety-two
in an old folks home
happy to be slightly
demented, my father-in-law
deceased and the Midwest
fifties hilltop house they built
soon to be sold.
Please don't go,
I say to everything
that has already gone:
ice candles we made
to line the driveway circle
on Christmas visits,
animal tracks in snow
viewed from the kitchen table,
sourdough pancakes, cardinals
at the bird feeder, ice fishing
on the Mississippi River with wind
chill fifty below zero, the bed
where my husband and I slept
in his boyhood room.
How foolish to imagine
I might have lived
any other life that wouldn't
arrive here, now
at exactly
this moment.

No Words

The neurologist goes through the usual rituals, taps knees, asks me to follow his finger . . . back and forth, up and down, watches me walk a straight line. All fine.
I'm going to say three words. I want you to repeat them. I do. For a few seconds he appears to be investigating something else, and then, looking me in the eye, he stops and says, *Say the words again.* Nothing . . . nothing comes to mind. My friend and I watch his face change, his voice soften as he fills out papers ordering an MRI. *Don't go alone,* he advises. Back home, within hours the phone rings. *It's a brain tumor.* The room starts to disappear. Again, no words. Only a feeling.

Only Days: Kalapana Coast, December, 2004

Alone on an asland
of volcanic fire
only days
before words
tell me death
is near. Pain
transcends all distraction.

By day
I listen to bamboo
trade wind music chime.
By night the breath
of breaching whales
echoes across the vast
emptiness of time
slowed down
to almost
nothing

While on a Mountaintop

In a Honolulu hospital my sons
hurry beside the gurney
as I roll toward the operating room.
I love you . . . all that's left to say.

As we approach the wide doors
a nurse in charge of IV drip tubes
says, in a teasing tone,
You're going to get drunk now.

It's so sudden. I never see the table
where my head's clamped down,
never hear a saw cutting into my skull,
never feel the tumor being sucked out.

Instead, darkness rises around me,
vast beyond knowing . . .
my body left behind.
In blackness, all those
who love me,

both the living and the dead,
surround me with grace.
Without seeing, I commune
with each and every one,

even a dog I love,
while my sons leave
and drive to an arboretum
on a verdant mountaintop,

where, amid exotic palms
and fragrant flowers,
they pray and wait
for the surgeon's call.

LISA SIMON

Cellar Peaches

I drag the sled along
with my thighs. I'm strapped
and bound for the
journey to your cabin, your
snow-tracks pulling downward
on my boots. Stripes in snow
break the field with my desire
to know what's below
snow, the beaming
bulbs sealed up in stark mud
brimming in closed fists.
Floating in my body
for days I come to you, and from
the sealed jar of peaches
comes my scent. The lid
sticks on the lip, then gives
with my pull, as I ask winter
to break its bright blind
force. Wet fingers
open me, beyond fission, beyond
any weather wreaking
havoc, smashing my house
to firesticks—hiss
on the wet snow. Cinders
are welcome too. I want
nothing but to have burned.

Faint Music Survives the Ocean

Write until the kids come home.
Try for the beauty that beams
far below the surface—there's the crash.
Inline skates thrown in the door bomb floorboards,

the ghost of design evaporates
from me. The soup is on,
the children's skulls intact
despite a day of dancing on skates,

menacing local streets—their veering
along oceanside cliffs is almost like
something I attempt
to call a reckless soul into form,

just enough wits to stay on pavement
most days, but how do I marry
adventure to care? I can't.
One cannot, it's maddening. The deafening

lull of wheels on bumpy pavement
is a background roar, a tide unlike
that of the ocean, a tide arranged
by none but muscle, luck, and grit.

I'll always wonder how fruitful
my pen would be without that music
(the skaters, TV, staccato of complaints,
the falsetto whine of kids' discord).

Because there is no life
without restraints, I crave it.
But time moves me. It's the season's end.
Soon comes the shift to winter rain,
the release from dead waves in the lagoon,
          the momentum.

LISA SIMON

In Season

Almost within reach, sky ornaments blazed mandarin,
and from far down the trail against the storm-grey
appeared thousands of leaf-fans, persimmon, as if eucalyptus
wore a head of fruit. Entering the grove, I saw the fans

peel off as butterflies, the Mardi Gras headpieces
unfeathering one by one in voluptuous,
unrushed motion: Monarchs hunting mates.
They spoke to me as they faltered

in mating: not so much of the wood rats,
hail, or freeze, but of the drenched
wings fanning in the sun, not the risk,
but the recovery from near-dead impulse. One,

a Japanese hairpiece clipped onto the handrail, unhooked
my breath out from under my wings. The fat
bread-fall of clenching pairs delivered me,
falling back into you for an instant. Taught

me to follow breath into the meeting
of bodies falling through space. Each
time the males missed a mate, swooping—
I felt my days narrow

into the eye of fortune's needle—whole days left
to successfully pair, and nights
for mating fervently up in treetops,
pared down to a breath over mudholes. No dog-heat

here, but I am dazed by the spectacle of pairs
wrestling and flipping—
urgent. Eucalyptus leaf-beds tremble with
the pairs who made it all the way back up

like drums signaling
the season of milkweed
and manzanita, the nursery and hatchery.
Males blade through air, stab,

and miss. Each female
has hundreds of eggs
that may never be touched, their tiny
fruit melting through the mudflat earth

as her wings thin under hail's wet weight,
disappear down earth's funnel as if
she never left that green casing, wings
shaken out, shouting.

Getting Pregnant After Forty

The late dahlias are brilliant
in the slant, sharp sun.

As potent as the earlies,
        more vivid in their urgency
        to spill laps of seeds
down their dresses.

The bumblebee wrestles
downed petals as if blind.
Uncertain, but trying every one.

Listening

At first it looked like you twisted your ankle
on loose trail rocks. But your marble eyes
were strangely washed out, gazing
at the blank sky above.
You were out cold, unresponsive,
then revived one long minute later.
Any precious reminder of the waking life,
and the welcome enormity
of you fastening a shoe: O! Truly divine
to see you sit upright, for, as the Torah says,
man doth not slither. Love, I've come to adore
each minor annoyance, the pitch
of your back-seat driving and mosquito music
now settles me. I check your nighttime breathing—
a mist of notes—somehow, my hand on your hip is best—
and relax. The air's grand mix, its tonic, travels
the proper course to inflate your sleeping belly,
though my own dreams will be lost
for a while—replaying the sonogram's
vivid testimony: that song
in action at the heart.

Sleepers

Of all relics to find
on the rubbled railroad lot: a fitting album,
Glenn Yarborough's "The Lonely Things."
The dazzle of cobalt blue
was a shock across the dusty yard.
I scrambled to pick it up—
a huge bite was missing from it.
Where did it fall, I wondered,
on the scale from black to platinum,
the color of the ones
who never made it?—or
simply the saddest single
about living the blues
at a wavelength not expressed by
common black vinyl?

So many discards here—the usual party-fight rubbish,
a block from the beach. A kid's unfinished
travel puzzle, bike tires, syringes,
wadded-up underpants, and condoms
in tired, gloomy puddles.

The riches here are vastly miniscule, evasive as dust,
and seem to waver and waft, transform
in the eyes of the seekers.
Worn spots of flattened grass
in the shape of sleepers—the ecstatic
can see the promise in the plain, can see
past the litter to the full sea
which holds and gives—gives,
but bears up with the massive weight
of its own wandering water
all these lonely things.

San Rafael Swell

This morning San Rafael Swell rises round,
damp from night's starry showers.

Fallen meteorites
knapped flint chip
up through sand
thrown from translucent
arrowheads.

Ascending potholes of deeper
and deeper pools
attract dragonfly, bird,
desert moth, canyon tree frog.

My self disappears, becomes
eyes and ears for sage
gusty spring air, cloud dancer,
grandmother pinion pine, her sand island
grandfather juniper root twists, swirls
from sandstone cracks,
exposes winter, summer, spring
one small branch alive, green.

Here, I do not abandon myself but belong
I know spring bloom, withering heat,
damage and change of a flash flood
undulation of this red rock body
in the brief neon pink sunsets.

I am welcomed home by clear, quiet
in the hum of simple endurance.

Wizard Watch

Wizard loves rocks, jade, garnet, the hardness of a rough diamond,
the brilliance that comes out of the earth formed under pressure
and heat. She conceives unlimited possibilities for magic and
movement in unexpected directions. When in me attitude or heart
may sour or shudder, Wizard waves an oak branch wand around
and around heart then body, glittering a reminder to lean carefully,
gently into life. Wizard knows healing sometimes comes winging
slowly to discover hidden doors behind boxes in a dark closet, or a
stairwell arcing up from a solid wall where none was before. Enter
me, I dare you! Find these stunning ripe worlds waiting, or . . .
catch a raft down Green River, heart pounding as I paddle hard to
see what's around the next bend. Wizard cackles, toothless, head
thrown back, warts dancing on the tip of her crooked nose, tangled
hair, falling over backwards, waving a gnarly finger of warning to
constantly stir and boil the pot, add sunrise beets, and parsnips,
something new every day. At night she demands poems sung to
the moonrise, air baths and blessing to all animals. Out come owls
with their yellow eyes, whoo-whooing, with Wizard flying me to
midnight blue then tucking me around a shooting star.

Persimmon Jam

Gifts from your Casserly Road tree
arrive in brown paper bags
glowing hearts, plump, heavy
and soft in the midst of winter
a promise of rich, slippery sweetness
delights to the tongue

I find myself loving you, smiling
as fingers separate pulp from skin
glistening lumps of persimmon color
to blend with lemon peel, lemon juice
a little honey added all dissolving
over simmering heat

I breathe in this fleshy fragrance
whisper a prayer to the kitchen goddess

Thank you for this great love we share
this mixing of ripe fruit in winter
this home we create every moment together
giving birth to our selves.

Los Campos

Along overgrown banks of the Colorado,
ghosts gather at old Spanish gypsy campos,
tamarisk scramble and sway
through late afternoon spots of sunlight.

We close our eyes, listen
for rhythm, swing of fiddle music,
see tall grasses bent over
by bare feet flying in a dance.

And to one side, a pile of stone
marks a burial
now bones, the last one
who remembers all the steps.

Operculum*

Small doors are everywhere on this Samoan beach
staring out and in at the same time, a white spiral, flat
smooth to touch, a surprising roundness,
fish eye, brown snakeskin texture.
Your spiral invites me to follow a fine line round
to your center, there is no place to go but reverse, I gather speed,
my finger flies from your surface past the moon, the stars
a spiral of purple-red galaxies sailing their dusty space tails.
For a moment I gaze into earth through you,
see my dear friend Gary resting in rooted flowers,
red ginger, plumeria, where he is still, at home,
becoming leaf and its necessary food.

Little operculum,
a sea snail's door, hinged to their shells,
a shield
that opens them to worlds of light, kelp forest, last night's hurricane,
the storms and tides of time, where thousands of doors are set free
to travel the morning's tide to settle on this beach.
Each one of hundreds of small doors before me
once held
something soft, pulled into its shell.
Once doors that served, opened then closed
over and over to what comes next,
another world, the one after
this one, the one Gary dances in,
his body's soft exit then nothing but the door left rolling,
rolling in the south sea, sand polished to silk.

———
*operculum: a lid or flap covering an aperture such as the shell cover
in sea snails or other mollusks.

All My Relations

Once upon a time we sang with the animals

We would listen to our own

far in the distance

then join in the chorus, mouths wide

to sound a stream of a capella coyote yips, our bodies

vibrating with the low moan of a she wolf

then up and over water in long lofted v's

a high sweet honking of snow geese

our heads lay back as they flew over us receiving,

returning the blessings of this song.

History Studies 1952

On Sunday, the A-bomb doesn't fall
but rain does, drops the shape of grapes
that burst themselves on the city.

On the kitchen wall, a photo of Uncle Jim in uniform
waving from a pontoon bridge over the Kumho River
on his way out to shoot Koreans.

On Monday, I go into the third grade to open
page one of the Catechism, "Who is God?"
then the picture book about how to hide
when the A-bomb falls
and how God and President Truman
would save our town and
me, under my desk repeating "Our Father,
whoartinheaven . . ."
until I die or until
President Truman sounds the all-clear siren
so I can walk home
and study page two of the Catechism.

On the way home I wade the edge
of the creek that rages
near the school grounds
perplexed
that this same water can find its way
into a grape, then a tear
and, after I push a large stone into the stream,
can so easily leap out of its trench
to wash away a playground.
How fragile history must be
when a single well-timed and placed stone
can kill a giant or re-route a river.

Tuesday, and no bomb blast in spite of our sins
but more rain arrives and a photo of
"Uncle Jim holding his ground." Dad explains,
"Wave after wave of Koreans attack him
and his machine gun."

I go to school anyway.

"God loves me," I sing,
as my friend Zimmer leads the charge, splashing
into the re-routed river that washes away layer after layer
of what remains of the school grounds.

No bomb falls, so Wednesday arrives
and more rain to swell the creek
that snakes under the classrooms.

"How much ground was lost?"
Father McLaughlin's eyes screw shut,
". . . one maybe two years of instruction."
he tells Sister Gerard, "The devil just got loose."

Zimmer's mom goes into the principal's office
and comes out holding Zimmer by the hand.
He waves good-bye and I'll never see my friend again—
nor Uncle Jim.

On Thursday, more rain.
We turn to page three of the Catechism.

My Friend Jacob

My friend Jacob went into mourning.
For three years he lived alone in the mountains
twenty miles from town.
It was Nevada City, that's where his wife left him

and where she lived, remarried,
kicked around the bars,
divorced,
then decided to come back to him.

Jacob woke that day and put on his lucky shirt,
the red Hawaiian he wore on their first date,
and holding a bunch of wild iris
he waited for her.

She never saw the Hawaiian shirt or the wild iris.
On the dirt road back,
a half-mile from their farm
she hung herself.

What is that rope
the one that comes out of the darkness
and jerks us
out of our innocence.

Teachers

Once upon a time
I shot a cat in the leg
because just the night before
my dad had shot one
to stop him from howling
after our cat Puff a runt
for reasons only Dad knew
that old tom had committed a sin
by just thinking or might soon commit one
if he didn't stop him
with a bullet through his head
which split open and pushed him back
over the fence into the neighbor's yard
which was where we played sometimes
but not too often
because the neighbor's daughter McGinty
we called her even though her real name was Patricia
was mentally retarded getting interested in boys
and one time asked me to pull my pants down
so she could look
which made the entire neighborhood nervous
because we were all Catholic maybe poor
and didn't know much
but we knew God hated stuff like that
and anybody who even thought about it
like cats
which is why I took my pellet rifle and went after the cat
sunning himself in his front yard
because he was a cat and having impure thoughts
about Puff or some other cat
and if he wasn't thinking them just then
he probably would that night
so I shot him in the leg so he would remember God
is watching and can strike you dead
anytime He wants and someday
will take aim and just when you least expect it
pull the trigger on you.

The Walk

Until today
I hadn't taken a walk with my father since I was ten.
We go down to the beach,
we talk about broken pipe and sand.

We don't waste time, we tell only the stories
about lost hunting dogs and heavy construction,
what and who we've worked with our whole lives,
dirt, earthmovers and my mother.

At the crest he stops, leans on his bamboo staff
to watch a distant cumulus cloud and a white heron
fishing in a ditch. Pulling himself up
he tells me his doctor found a cancer.

A moment is an odd thing—
if we lived forever, we'd miss it.

Construction

a love story

Coffee and donuts, KPIG Radio
it's another 6:30 sunrise, loading trucks
with shovels, stakes, header boards, sledge,
and for the Wacker Tamper, we bend together and lift.
Who knows about tomorrow, but today
we're together. I am one of them.
Nobody told us in a couple years
we'd all be paying child support
or that a month after Swede retires
his heart would stop, or about Granger's cool wife, Mary,
who'd split on him. Nobody told us
he'd disappear in his trailer behind the Torch Light Motel
and drink himself to death.
"Don't sweat small stuff," he'd say.
At work what matters: I am one of them.
We weren't ugly, just worn ragged
by Marlboros, insults, rattling red diesel cans, and loud talk
who's late, who's no fucking good,
who knows his ass from a hole in the ground,
who's breaking, who isn't.
Love is a strange language. I am one of them.

Work, a bunch of happy bullshit no one quits
because there's nowhere to go. 7:30, strap on your tool belt
slam the rest of your coffee, slap Chino, "Vayamos!" & grin.
Chino! his scraggled Foo-Man-Choo, silly,
the best screed man we'd ever known & nobody forgets
his wife and five kids who got head on-ed by a semi,
all killed. It's together we carried their coffins,
downed some beers and dropped Chino at his empty house.
Now we were his home, the ones who read his language
the ever-present cigarette, his smile, his worn-out shoes.
Chino misses a half-day's work
then shows up, shovel in hand. Whatever his reasons,
I am one of them.
I am one of them.

Part newlywed, part songstress, part mother, part Pushcart Prize nominee, the poet **Julia Alter-Canvin** now resides in Venice Beach. Her firstborn book is *Walking the Hot Coal of the Heart* (Hummingbird Press, 2004). Be on the lookout for Julia's forthcoming recordings, soothing fusions of poetry and jazz.

Poet and physicist **Len Anderson** is the author of *Affection for the Unknowable* (Hummingbird Press, 2003). His poems have appeared in *Bellowing Ark, Caesura, DMQ Review, Good Times, Monterey Poetry Review, The Montserrat Review, Porter Gulch Review, Quarry West, The Sand Hill Review, Sarasota Review of Poetry,* and *The Anthology of Monterey Bay Poets 2004.* He is a winner of the Dragonfly Press Poetry Competition and the Mary Lönnberg Smith Poetry Award.

Virgil Banks scrabbles for poems.

Dane Cervine's book *What A Father Dreams,* and recent chapbooks are available from the author at his website: http://danecervine.typepad.com/. Over 100 of Dane's poems have appeared in print, including the *The Hudson Review, The Sun,* and various anthologies. His work was chosen by Adrienne Rich as the 2005 National Writers Union winner, and by Tony Hoagland as a finalist for the 2005 Wabash Prize for Poetry. Dane was the Porter Gulch Review 2005 Poet of the Year. His new book is *The Jeweled Net of Indra* published by Plain View Press in 2007.

Jenny D'Angelo has been writing since her first poems appeared on hand-made greeting cards at age 6. Born in Massachusetts, she lived and studied in Europe before moving to California in 1977. Her work has appeared in *Bellowing Ark* and *Only the Sea Keeps*. Her spoken word CD, *Light from the Tip of the Tongue,* sells internationally. (You can order it at www.nlpu.com/Jenny.) A longtime student of spirituality, healing and light, Jenny lives in a little bungalow by the sea, with her urban chickens and their lovely blue-green eggs.

Guarionex Delgado: Long-haired brown male. 60ish. Member of the divine creation. Nemesis of church and state and corporate power. Friend of saints, sinners, pagans, prophets, Jesus, Buddha, and Mohammed. Long live the spirit of life. Long live Coyote. August 2006.

Kathleen Flowers is a bilingual educator. Her poems have been published in *The Anthology of Monterey Bay Poets 2004, Porter Gulch Review, The Matrix* and *Moments in the Journey.* She is a winner of the Mary Lönnberg Smith Poetry Award.

Robin Lysne is the author of *Heart Path: Learning to Love Yourself and Listening to Your Guides* (poetry and prose, Blue Bone Books, 2007), and *Dancing Up the Moon* (poetry and prose) and *Living a Sacred Life* (prose), both published by Conari Press. Her poems have appeared in *Porcupine, North American Review* and several anthologies. She has shared her poetry in readings such as In Celebration of the Muse, and around the San Francisco Bay Area. She works as a substance abuse counselor for PVPSA, and is also a medium and intuitive. Her website is: www.thecenterforthesoul.com

Joanna Martin is the author of *The Meaning of Wings* (Hummingbird Press, 2003). She received her BA in Literature and Creative Writing from San Francisco State University. She has been a nurse for 19 years at Dominican Hospital, and works in Cardiac Care. Her work has been published in *Porter Gulch Review* and *Quarry West*. She is a winner of the Mary Lönnberg Smith Poetry Award.

Phyllis Mayfield lives in the Santa Cruz Mountains. A poet for 27 years, a love poet for 14, her work has appeared in *Women Artists' Datebook, Porter Gulch Review, Santa Cruz Sentinel,* the Poet's Eye Artist's Tongue art exhibit, and she has read at In Celebration of the Muse and on KPIG radio. She hosts the monthly Verbal Moonshine reading and is finishing her memoir, *Gazebo.*

Maggie Paul holds an MFA in Poetry from Vermont College. Her work has appeared in *Poetry Miscellany, Smartish Pace, the Sarasota Review, Rattle,* and other journals. Maggie is a co-founder of Poetry Santa Cruz. Her chapbook, *Stones from the Baskets of Others,* was published by Black Dirt Press in 2002.

Stuart Presley is a poet, husband, carpenter and photographer in search of the ineffable. He wrote his first poem at age twelve. Later poems have been published in California and the Southwest. Currently living on the north coast of Santa Cruz County with the love of his life, he communes with bobcats and silence.

Having fled the Kansas of her childhood, **Carol Rodriguez** (formerly Housner) has explored the Oz of poetry for the past twelve years. Mother to three, sister to four and friend to a myriad, she presently lives in Aptos with her two sons. Because prairie sun still lives in her heart, she has recently donned her ruby slippers again, but remains a huge fan of flying monkeys.

Joan Safajek is a retired psychotherapist and former English teacher who lives with a Tibetan puppy called *Kaimu*. Her poems have been published in *The Anthology of Monterey Bay Poets 2004* and *Porter Gulch Review*. She is also a recipient of the Mary Lönnberg Smith Poetry Award. Following in the footsteps of Zen poet Ryokan, her elder life with children and grandchildren *is like an old hermitage . . . simple and quiet.*

Lisa Simon is a writer, teacher and singer whose love of language was nurtured in her birthplace of Birmingham, Alabama. She holds an MFA in Writing and a BA in English. She has read at In Celebration of the Muse and her poems have appeared in *Quarry West, Porter Gulch Review* and elsewhere. She lives in Santa Cruz County with her husband and daughter.

Robin Straub lives free in the Utah high desert of the Colorado Plateau. She is a full time plein air oil painter and a once-upon-a-time in another life poet, teacher and volunteer. Every day she is astonished by the natural beauty and kind friends that surround her.

Philip Wagner. After all these years, still an idealist. With wine, a philosopher. One-time documentary maker and editor of ACT in Paris. Hosted the National Writer's Union poetry reading for four years, co-produced the NWU poetry show on local television and co-founded Poetry Santa Cruz. Teaches poetry in county mental health program. Lectures on Mythology, Art, and Psychology. Published in *Porter Gulch Review, Quarry West, The Anthology of Monterey Bay Poets 2004* and has two chapbooks, *Wild Horses Are Always in Heaven* and *Found Poems*.

History of the Emerald Street Poets

We originally met in Joseph Stroud's poetry class at Cabrillo College in Aptos, California. Some of us had been with him several semesters. In June of 1995 Joe announced that he was going to take a year's sabbatical and no class would be offered in the fall.

At the end-of-term celebration the following week, we were all talking about how disappointed we were that we would no longer be able to have the class discussions or receive ideas to improve our writing.

Phil Wagner suggested that we start our own critique group. He started a sign-up sheet for anyone who wanted to join. We ended up with over twenty names. We signers immediately gathered and decided to meet on alternate Thursday nights at Robin Straub's house on Emerald Street in Capitola. We were pleased to have eight to ten poets come each time to give feedback on our poems and celebrate our creativity. Now, with some new members, we continue to meet every other Thursday.

In 1997, Phyllis Mayfield had a weekend writing workshop at her Santa Cruz Mountain acres the poets call "Paradise." We still gather for three overnights a year. We are truly in Paradise when we write in view of the still-bearing century-old apple orchard which appears on the front and back covers.